Elwood's Bath

Written by Larry Dane Brimner • Illustrated by Teri Weidner

The Child's World

Published in the United States of America by The Child's World®
PO Box 326 • Chanhassen, MN 55317-0326
800-599-READ • www.childsworld.com

Reading Adviser

Cecilia Minden-Cupp, PhD, Director of Language and Literacy, Harvard University Graduate School
of Education, Cambridge, Massachusetts

Acknowledgments

The Child's World®: Mary Berendes, Publishing Director

Editorial Directions, Inc.: E. Russell Primm, Editorial Director and Project Manager; Katie Marsico,
Associate Editor; Judith Shiffer, Assistant Editor; Matt Messbarger, Editorial Assistant

The Design Lab: Kathleen Petelinsek, Design and Art Production

Library of Congress Cataloging-in-Publication Data

Brimner, Larry Dane.
   Elwood's bath / written by Larry Dane Brimner ; illustrated by Teri Weidner.
      p. cm. — (Magic door to learning)
   Summary: Young Elwood prepares for bathtime as he adds his favorite playmates, including
eight large elephants, to the water.
   ISBN 1-59296-521-0 (library bound : alk. paper) [1. Baths—Fiction. 2. Addition—Fiction.]
I. Weidner, Teri, ill. II. Title.
   PZ7.B767Elw 2005
   [E]—dc22   2005005370

A book is a door, a magic door.
It can take you places
you have never been before.
Ready? Set?
Turn the page.
Open the door.

Now it is time to explore.

3

"It's bathtime," Mama told Elwood.

4

"I can do it myself," Elwood said.
"Are you sure?" asked Dad.

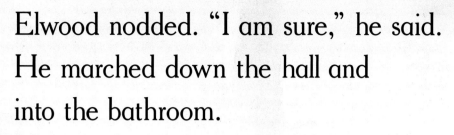

Elwood nodded. "I am sure," he said.
He marched down the hall and
into the bathroom.

He looked in the tub,
but it was empty. So
he got 2 yellow ducks
and put them in the tub.

9

"There," he said, but
something wasn't right.

What was a bath without
his favorite 4 spouting whales?

"Okay," said Elwood.
He was ready for
a splash, when he
remembered something
else. He never took a bath
without his 6 bright boats.

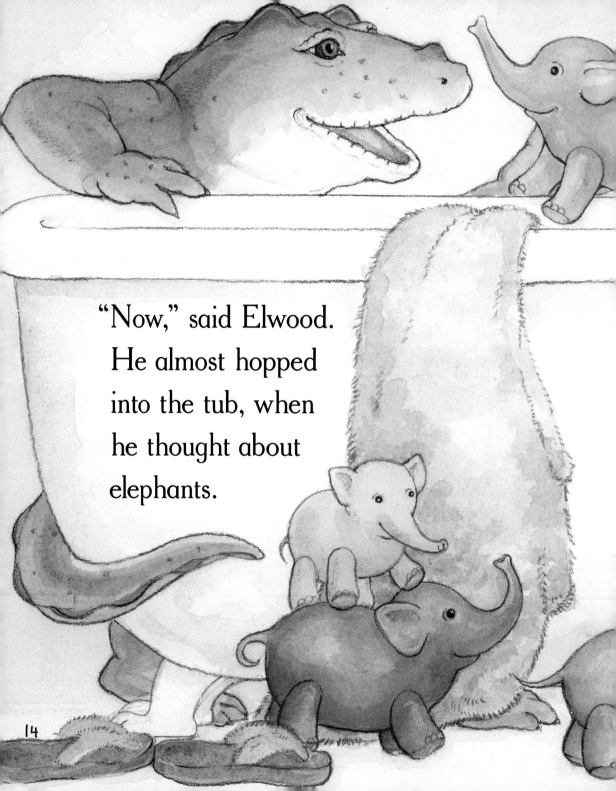

"Now," said Elwood.
He almost hopped
into the tub, when
he thought about
elephants.

14

He had 8 large elephants.
They all loved a good bath!

"Ready," said Elwood,
and sat down in the tub.
But then he got a funny feeling.
Had he forgotten something?

"My crocodiles!"
said Elwood. So
10 toothy crocodiles
tumbled into the tub.
"Perfect. It's full,"
said Elwood.
"And now it's bathtime."

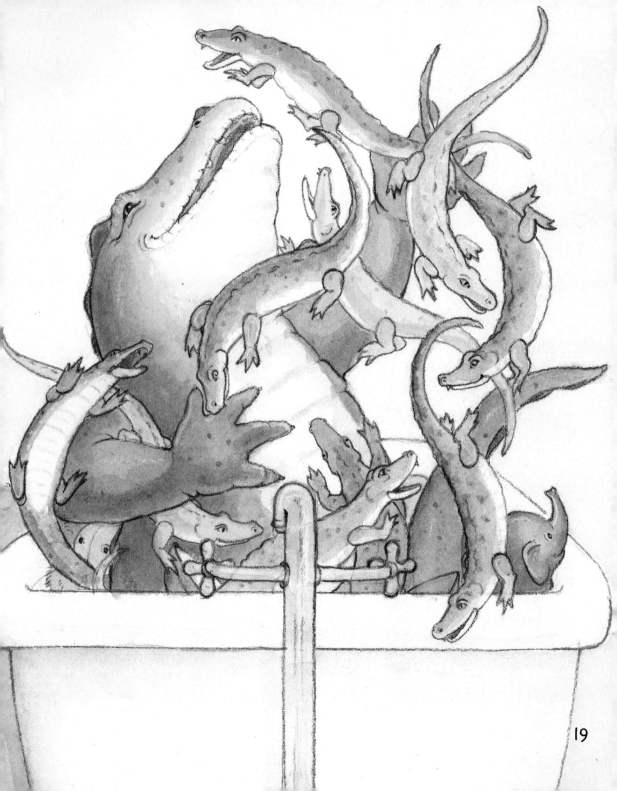

He settled in among
2 yellow ducks,
4 spouting whales,
6 bright boats,
8 large elephants, and
10 toothy crocodiles,
when he remembered
one other thing.

Our story is over, but there is still much to explore beyond the magic door!

How do you get ready for a bath? Before your next bath, count all the various items you bring along with you. Be sure to include toys, your towel, washcloth, bathrobe, and anything else you might use. Are your arms as full as Elwood's?

These books will help you explore at the library and at home:
Cousins, Lucy. *Maisy Takes a Bath.* Cambridge, Mass.: Candlewick Press, 2000.
Rylant, Cynthia, and Isidre Mones (illustrator). *Puppy Mudge Takes a Bath.* New York: Simon & Schuster Books for Young Readers, 2002.

About the Author

Larry Dane Brimner is an award-winning author of more than 120 books for children. When he isn't at his computer writing, he can be found biking in Colorado or hiking in Arizona. You can visit him online at *www.brimner.com.*

About the Illustrator

Teri Weidner grew up in Fairport, New York, where she spent much of her free time drawing horses and other animals. Today, she is delighted to have a career illustrating books for children. Her latest, *Look Both Ways* by Diane Z. Shore and Jessica Alexander, is about an impulsive little squirrel. She lives in Portsmouth, New Hampshire with her husband and a menagerie of pets.